Relationships Unscripted

By Ben Winter and Tara Hedberg

Relationships Unscripted

Relationships are Improvised.

Learn the Rules.

Be Successful.

ISBN-10:   0-9992944-2-3

ISBN-13: 978-0-9992944-2-0

Special thanks to:

Patricia Winter
Mandell Winter Jr.
PSI Seminars
Madcap Theater, Westminster, CO
Rodents of Unusual Size Improv Comedy Troupe

3

Chapter 1

Where's Your Script?

Wake up!!! Quick, read your script! You know, the one for the entire day. Quick!!! You have 5 minutes to read it and memorize it because you have a day to get to. So not only do you need to memorize your schedule, but all of the unanticipated changes shifts and problems that will arise; every conversation dialogue needs to be memorized, every second planned, Oh, and make sure you follow it exactly!!!

Yikes! If you had to do that every morning that would suck. Plus, it wouldn't even be possible. You literally cannot read an entire days' worth of dialog, memorize it, and perform it exactly. Especially when nobody is doing their parts according to your script.

Guess what? We live in a world that is improvised every minute of every day. There are no exceptions. The problem is that nobody realizes it and even fewer understand that good improv follows some very simple and very powerful rules.

Let's look at a popular TV show, "Whose Line Is It Anyway?" This show was successful because the improv artists on stage were all following the same set of rules. If they weren't, the show wouldn't be good and it wouldn't have stayed on the air very long.

Have you ever been to local improv show? Did it suck? For example, was there one performer who was very funny, but the scenes never seemed to go anywhere? Did the performers seem like they were uncomfortable with each other? Did one performer seem to not jive with the rest of the group? If so, it was likely that one or more of the people on stage weren't following the rules. But if you were left in awe by the performance, wondering how they did that, how they could come up with what they did on the spot, you can bet that they were all following the rules of improv.

Let's take a step back and define improv. The improv I am referring to here isn't the standup comedy variety but rather the kind of improv where a group of people work together to come up with a good story (long or short) without knowing how they are going to get there, what they are even starting with, and without preparing for it.

Here is the dictionary.com definition...

the art or act of improvising, or of composing, uttering, executing, or arranging anything without previous preparation

This is exactly what we do on a daily basis in everyday life. We don't prepare our dialog. We don't prepare who we are going to meet and when we are going to meet them. Especially in relationships. Improv is the part where nothing goes as planned.

Think of it like this: You are called out of the audience, told to stand up on stage, and then told……..GO!!!! For most people, they would freeze, go into shock, freak out, and possibly run away. After all the #1 fear in the US is public speaking.

Only, you are called to the stage every moment of every day and you are only given the information available to you in that moment.

How can we possibly handle this on a daily basis? Well, we have adapted over time to sort of, stumble our way through it. We have found patterns and techniques that seem to work to get us by. But is that thriving? Is that effective in getting what you want? Is that helping you achieve your dreams and goals?

What if there was a better way?

An easier way?

Chapter 2

The Game

You have probably heard of "the game of life". Life being referenced as a game is very common. Don't all games come with a set of rules? Doesn't following those rules make it easier to win? To have fun? To feel involved? Isn't there a sense of freedom with knowing that you know what is going on?

Let's look at a game like chess. There are rules. Certain pieces can only move in certain ways. If both players move the pieces how they see fit, then how do you know if you are winning? How do you know if you lost? How do you form a strategy when there is nothing to work with? There is simply a lot of chaos, fighting, misunderstanding, confusion, and ultimately a hatred of the game. You want to stop playing.

When the rules of chess are followed, you know that the other player is following them when they move the pieces accordingly. You can have fun. Get creative. Form a strategy. And then you know when you win.

How about a team sport, like hockey? Would it be very fun to watch if everyone on the ice was following their own set of rules? How could the referees enforce those rules? Isn't it likely that someone is going to get hurt? And if they do, is that a penalty when there aren't any rules to follow? Nobody would stay on the ice and play. Everyone would get angry and frustrated! The fans would leave. It just wouldn't work out.

When hockey is played and everyone is following the rules, everyone has more fun. You know what you can do. You know what you shouldn't do. You can challenge yourself to be better within the confines of the rules. You know the consequences when you do something that isn't allowed. A team can work together to ultimately triumph and win the game. They can create a strategy that allows them to be effective.

Kids crack me up because they start out without knowledge of rules and how to setup the games they play. They will start playing a game and every time something isn't going their way, they add a rule. They change the rules. They make the rules for others but not themselves. As an adult, playing with a child who is making up the rules as they go along, becomes infuriating and ridiculous. I stop the game. I ask for the rules. I ask if those rules can stay the same without being changed for the rest of the game. I do this so that I know the boundaries in which we are playing. A great example is a Nerf gun battle. We load guns with foam darts and the game starts. Then, when I get hit with a bullet I am dead. Great. That must mean when you get hit you're dead. But when I hit my son with a dart it now becomes three times before you are dead. But then I get hit a second time and I am dead. But…wait…didn't you just change the rules? Don't those apply to everyone? Let's stop this game and figure this out before I just walk away because it isn't fun anymore.

A better way of putting it is, **setting the expectations**.

But wait! What about all of those "relationships rules"? Like "calling 2 days after the first date." Or "The guys pays on the first date." Aren't those already defined?

No. They aren't. Nobody has the same set of rules and their definitions are different for each made up rule that nobody knows about. Unless your date is overwhelming and shares all of their rules and expectations on the first date (or even before the first date) you will never know their rules (expectations).

Before we get too far…this book isn't just about dating and romantic relationships…so stay tuned.

The game of relationships is no different. There are rules to follow, but you don't need both people to know the rules to be successful. We'll explain later.

The game of improv has a set of rules. Guess what? Improv and relationships have the same set of rules. Why doesn't everyone know these rules? Because most people have never learned the rules so they aren't able to teach those rules to others. Most people are afraid of "improv" and don't take classes. Some people may read about the rules of improv but misinterpret them. Another problem people have today is a short attention span, we want to know the answer NOW, want the results NOW, in improv we want the laugh NOW. People also don't necessarily relate the rules of performance improv to the improv of relationships.

The game of relationships, when following the rules, can lead to more fun, happiness, success, excitement, understanding, opportunity, caring, sharing, trust, and love.

When everything around you is crumbling, wouldn't it be nice to know how to laugh at it and put on the "let's play" hat rather than freaking out and running away? Wouldn't it be nice to know the set of rules in which to play in at that moment?

Rather than ever getting insulted again, you can see things from a different perspective, and act in a way where you have fun with the insult rather than getting insulted?

Wouldn't it be more fun to work with your relationships to solve problems before they escalate and end badly?

It can happen.

And this is how it happened…

Chapter 3

How This Concept Came To Be

I went into my adolescence with no self-confidence. That carried through college and into my early 20s. Then I was introduced to a personal growth seminar. I wanted one thing, to be in a relationship. I thought I would come out of college with an idea of who I wanted to marry. I didn't even date in college. That's how low my self-confidence was. When the seminar company said "what if you can have better relationships?" I handed them a check and never looked back. I spent 8 years learning, volunteering, and getting the knowledge so that things could be different. But all I was doing was learning. I wasn't really implementing that knowledge to a degree where things changed all that much.

Yes, I eventually got my first real relationship. Yes, I dated. I even got married and had a kid. But

I was still unhappy. Prior to marriage, I followed my girlfriend (soon to be fiancé) to an improv class. Something I had always wanted to do but again, lacked the self-esteem to do so. I FELL IN LOVE with improv! It was so freeing when they shared the rules and the structure of improv. It took so much pressure off of the concept of improv. I was set free with some new found knowledge.

Imagine that!! Rules being something that takes the pressure away and sets you free rather than confining you to a box.

The class lasted 6 weeks and then we got to perform for friends and family. I couldn't get enough. I wanted more. I finally felt at home. I took the class again. I took the advanced class. I took an acting class. And it was there, in the acting class, that I met someone who would help change my life for good. She told me I should come audition with her improv troupe. I did. Thank you Jessica.

It was scary meeting a group of people I didn't know. But I also knew, if I just followed the rules I learned, everything would be great. And it was.

Except, it didn't go as planned. Imagine that. The leader of the troupe said I would be a better fit with a different troupe. "But, my friend is in this troupe..." I thought. Talk about getting thrown for a loop.

Here I was again, being scared, going to meet people I didn't know, to do something I found to be fun.

Over ten years later, still with the same improv troupe, having my background of personal growth knowledge, having quit my nine year corporate job, having had a child, having started my own company, and getting a divorce, I found myself in the darkest place of my life. I started meditating on a regular basis. I started doing things for me again. And during a meditation, my life's purpose, my life's passion, was shown to me in an actionable way. I saw Success Improv. I saw a way to help others. I saw a way to put my passion to action. I found my way.

While I got the spark I needed to move forward, I didn't have all of the answers. I started writing things down. Formulating the system. And it was during that process that I realized that I couldn't do it alone as effectively as I could with a team. With someone who had a very similar background. Someone who had the same set of rules that I did.

And that was when I turned to the most obvious candidate, Tara Hedberg. She did the same personal growth work that I did. She had pieces of the puzzle that I didn't have. She and I had been performing improv together for years. We already had the trust necessary to pull this off with great ease and excitement.

When I shared the concept, Tara didn't hesitate. She saw the value, the vision, the passion. She knew it would be as successful as I saw it in my vision. And because we had similar backgrounds, it came together with little effort.

After a couple trial runs, bringing in some businesses coaches, and fine tuning the product, it became "show ready." Ready for the world. After running through the system a few more times we knew it was dialed in and completely effective.

And now, you can reap the benefits of **decades** of work.

So, what now?

What are the rules of relationships?

What are the rules of improv?

Chapter 4

What Are The Rules Of Improv?

The rules of improv are a foundation that you use underneath all of your actions. When you have a strong foundation, you can build the biggest sky scrapers. You can withstand earthquakes, tsunamis, hurricanes, and so much more. When your foundation is set, you are so much more powerful. With the right foundation, all things are possible and also much easier to attain.

The first thing you need to know is that there are a lot of rules of improv. But you don't need to know all of them to be successful. We have found the top 5 that can be the easiest to follow and the most effective in life. These 5 rules are the foundation that you can use for anything life throws at you. These 5 rules can help with your relationships and so much more.

The 5 main rules of improv are:

Don't Deny

Yes, And…

Be Specific

Focus on the Present

Trust

Seems simple enough, yes? But most people don't know exactly what these rules mean when it comes to improv. When it comes to life and relationships. When you just see the rules in their shortest form you are left to interpret them how you see fit, which ultimately changes the rules. We can't stop here. We have to explain the rules so that you are clear about the meaning of these rules. We have to set the boundaries of these rules. Set the expectations. And in the end, not only do we need to set the expectations of each rule, we also have to show you how they all work together. How one is no more important than any of the others.

Let us being with rule number 1...

Chapter 5

Rule #1

Don't Deny

The first rule of improv – Don't Deny

Ask any improv performer and they will happily agree that this is the number one rule of improv. They might call it something else, like "agree with", "agree", "say yes". They might even call our second rule "Yes, And…" the number one rule, but "Yes, And…" is something more. We'll explain later.

It all comes down to "**Accepting What Is**".

What does this mean?

In the world of performance improv, it means accepting what is given to you by the other performers, what is given to you by the audience, what is given to you by the scenario, what is given to you by your surroundings. It is simply saying to yourself, "This is what I have at this very moment and there is no denying that it is this way. It is what it is. Things are as they are."

An example of performance improv might go something like this:

Two male actors walk out on stage and the first one says, "Mom, I broke my arm today." Well, it's clear to everyone at that very moment that the other person on stage is a guy. So what is he going to do? Well, if that actor is following the rules, he is going to accept what is given to him. In this case he is given the role of mom for the scene. If the actor doesn't deny this fact, they can move forward and create magic on stage. Everyone else will also accept that this is now that guy's role.

But what if he DENIES the role? By denying the role he breaks the scene. Nobody knows what is going on. The audience becomes lost. The actors become unbelievable. The other actor doesn't know what to do next. Everything, momentarily, is in chaos. Everyone is confused. Nobody knows what to do next because the rules have just been broken.

This leads to a really bad scene and ultimately a really bad show. Had the actor simply followed the rules, all would be moving forward in a scene that could end up being regarded as brilliant, leaving the audience in awe of what just happened, and everyone having more fun.

Okay, that is improv. But what about REAL LIFE RELATIONSHIPS?

In our relationships we are constantly met with situations we don't care for. Disagreements. Misunderstanding. Fights. Mismatched personalities. Conflict. Lack of passion. Lack of energy. And so much more.

We are also presented with situations that we love. Although, it is really easy not to deny those situations so we aren't going to focus on them here.

A lot of people dwell on something that happened once, many years ago, and are still in denial about what happened. Guess what? It happened. Otherwise you wouldn't be able to dwell on it. Accepting that it happened gives you power to move on. Acceptance is a very very VERY powerful tool! There probably isn't a psychiatrist on the planet who wouldn't agree that acceptance of what is (or what was) is necessary for healing. For moving forward.

Accepting what is, creates a moment of peace. A calmness. A place where there are possibilities and not limitations.

By now you are asking for the how. How do I accept what is when it is so horrible? How do I accept what is when there are ramifications to what just happened?

The answer is simple and yet so hard. It is as simple as taking a deep breath, taking that one moment (a 3-second period of time) and simply saying, yes, that just happened. Or yes, that is where we are. Or yes, this is what it is.

We as humans are so fast at reacting that we don't even give ourselves the 3 seconds, the single moment in time, to do something different.

But when you can take a moment for everything that happens that you don't like, you give yourself awareness, which leads to understanding, which leads to peace of mind.

When you can stop and "yes, this shitty thing just happened" and leave it at that, for 3 seconds, for a single moment, you can flow into rule number two and do something about it.

You can stop in the moment and just start laughing rather than crying.

You can stop in the moment and reflect on how you just got to that moment.

You can stop and not react.

You can respond.

And how do you respond?

Chapter 6

Rule #2

Yes, And…

The second rule of improv – Yes, And...

As we said before, some schools of improv call this the first rule. So why did we break it out and make it its own rule? Well, let's break apart these two words. *Yes* is the accepting and the positive side of *Don't Deny*. The second word in this rule is very important. *And*, is a positive furtherance of the accepting of what is. Unfortunately, it is possible to throw a *But* into this rule in the place of the *And*, which does not create good Improv. These two words create two different meanings. Let's talk about them and how they work differently.

The word *"But"* negates what's in front of it. Think of it like this, "I love you, but..." doesn't sound very good. It sounds like there are conditions to the "what is" statement of "I love you". It basically says, I have conditions about my love, or my love for you was interrupted by something.

The word *"And"* adds to what's in front of it. Our example of "I love you, and..." doesn't take away from the "what is" factor. The love is still there. The *"And"* implies that there is more.

Putting it into a full example:

"I love you, but I am really upset about what you did today."

vs

"I love you, and I am really upset about what you did today."

The second one has a feel of hope. Great, you still love me. And now I know that that love is in jeopardy because of my actions (or your interpretation of my actions). The first statement implies that it isn't in jeopardy, it is already lost. And how do you grow from there?

In performance improv this rule helps to move the scene forward. It adds to the scene. As said in one of my favorite movies, Deadpool, "It might further the plot". Let's go back to our example of "Mom, I broke my arm today."

If the actor does a "Yes, but" the scene will again be in chaos.

If the response is, "Oh, you're arm is broken, but it doesn't look broken." Now nobody believes it is broken and it negates what the first actor did to establish the scene. They accepted being the mom (in this instance) but didn't add to the scene. Instead, the actor took something away.

What if they added to the scene? What are the possibilities?

They could have said, "Oh honey, at least you got a bright red cast. Red is your favorite color." In that instance they added that it had already been fixed. And that they like the color red. They added to the scene to help it progress.

Another approach could be to act as though it's the worst thing that ever happened and start freaking out, "Oh No! We have to get to the hospital quick! This can't be happening! Not my child! Does it hurt? Do you want a bandage? What do we do? Does your dad know? How did this happen?" and so on. This approach would add to the scene subjectively by showing how crazy the mom is and how she handles a situation. Again, this moves the scene forward. The actors can add to what has been added. And, they have to accept the new information as "what is". They must not deny the new information.

Rule number 1 and rule number 2 are intertwined. They often play off of one another on a moment by moment basis.

As long as you don't negate the acceptance you can move forward.

What about life you ask?

Let's look at something called brainstorming. It's a tool that people use to come up with ideas to help them solve a problem. It usually involves multiple people and it can be done by an individual person. We are going to use the group example first.

A group of family members are deciding the best thing to do at the family reunion. They have decided to sit down and do some brainstorming. If everyone lets the ideas flow and nobody's ideas are negated, then everyone feels like they can share.

If everyone who offers an idea is shot down by someone else in the room, how likely are they to share any more ideas that come up. The brainstorming comes to an end rather quickly, there is resentment in the room, and a lack of trust and understanding for each other.

How often in life do we not speak up or share ideas because we are afraid of them being shot down? How much does this stop us? Nobody wins. Give it a try.

Given enough time, and enough *"Yes, and's"* that group could come up with some of the best ideas any family has ever had for a family reunion. This becomes a much more fun exercise.

This rule of improv might be the most crucial for innovation. For creativity. For moving forward and busting through an obstacle.

As an individual, you can brainstorm your own ideas. The key is to not shoot down your own ideas. Just write them out and don't dismiss anything that you write. Just keep coming up with ideas. Come up with ideas about ideas. Just let it flow until you have something you can work with. And if you run out of ideas and it doesn't seem to have accomplished anything, take a break and come back later. Again, the key is to not make yourself wrong about your ideas.

Speaking of making people or yourself wrong…

Chapter 7

Yes, And Part 2

This rule of improv is perfect for making someone wrong. Bear with us here...

Who likes to be wrong? Not many people. Who likes to be pointed out that they are wrong? Even fewer people. Most people can accept being wrong when they realize it on their own. When it is pointed out they will fight tooth and nail to not be wrong. This rule is perfect for showing people they are wrong by providing information to them so that they come to that conclusion on their own.

In a more positive frame of reference, this is about education. It is about providing more information so those involved can make a more accurate decision.

For example, in improv, suppose a pair of players are on stage and playing a scene that is just not going anywhere, another player has the chance to come in and excite the scene. Now to do this in a way that supports the scene and the original players, the new player does not fight what has been started.

A scene that was established with two people cooking, very politely and calmly, can be energized by a third player running on and saying "Guys, I know you want these meals to be perfect, and I am so glad you are committed to greatness, and the customers are about to riot if I don't bring them some food." All of a sudden the perfectionist chefs have an exciting scene to play with, the conflict comes between perfectionism and timeliness, which could be fun for the audience because they recognize that struggle.

In contrast the third player could run into the scene yelling at the players to get the led out because people are starving, and while it may get a quick laugh, the other players will be embarrassed and frustrated and the group dynamic will be damaged. Then, instead of playing with a fact of modern life, it becomes a fight between the primary players and the interloper, which is usually very unentertaining. There are plenty of outlets to see people scream at each other and it is simply not funny or entertaining.

In fact the "adding to a scene in need" is the best way for a group of improvers to grow as a unit.

Now, how this rule relates to real life. Let's say someone is telling you that you are doing something incorrectly. How do they know? Perhaps you have more information than they do? You could just start arguing about it, or you can do something different. You can educate the person who is telling you that you are doing something wrong. You can say something like, "I can see how you might think I am doing it wrong, and have you thought about x, y, and z?" or "I can see your view point, and I know the way I am doing it is another way to accomplish the same goal."

Maybe it is something as simple as washing the dishes. If you were washing the dishes and someone said you are washing them wrong, you can respond by asking them how they think the dishes should be done, you can tell them that you see how they might think that, and that the end result of clean dishes will be accomplished either way, or a combination of both approaches.

By providing more information, the person was able to change their mind without feeling like they were made wrong. Now that they have the same information, that person can see that it isn't a problem to keep working in what was perceived as an incorrect approach.

Another example comes from some of our workshops. When working in education, teachers sometimes come across the issue of seeing different results from the students than their parents see. Parents may come in with statements like "He never behaves poorly at home, he is my little angel." Arguing with a parent who has this belief is not going to go anywhere.

However if you follow rule 2 you can agree; "I am sure he is an angel at home, and it must be something about being in a group of kids that gets him to misbehave. How could we solve this?" Not only is the parent not made wrong, they have been invited into creating the solution.

Yes, And helps to further knowledge, education, agreement, and understanding. Couldn't we all use more understanding in life?

When you *"Yes, and"* you must …

Wait for it…

Getting closer…

Maybe take a break?

Nah…

Proceed to the next page now?

Chapter 8

Rule #3

Be Specific

The third rule of improv – Be Specific

Be specific. Well, if that isn't obvious right out of the gate, let us be more specific. And the best way we have found is to provide examples. Let's start with a performance improv example.

Two people enter the stage and one says "I spilled it." Well, I can tell you right away, the other actor is left with the burden of setting the stage for the scene. What did they spill? Why does it matter? Who are they? Who are you? So many questions left open. The audience doesn't know what is going on. The actors don't know what is going on. It is a horrible place to start an improv scene. The first actor may have an idea of what the scene is about. Perhaps they spilled a glass a milk in their mind, but they didn't share their expectations of the scene by being specific from the start. When the second actor doesn't go with that expectation, it could cause friction. It could cause denial. It could kill the scene before it ever gets going.

What could be done to improve the open line in the scene? How about the first actor coming out and saying, "Honey, I was painting the living room and I spilled the paint on our new carpet." Well, that picture is painted so well, that any actor, any person really, could *"yes, and"* the scene and carry it forward for a long period of time. There are so many directions the other actor could go. There are so many options. The expectations of the scene, who everyone is, the scenario, are all set.

A real world example would be the "Honey, please take out the trash." scenario. That's a pretty specific request, right? Well, that depends on the underlying expectations.

As you may have guessed, this rule is more about expectations (known and unknown) than it is about anything else. And by *being specific*, you get to set those expectations clearly.

In the "take out the trash" scenario, we are going to assume it is the wife asking the husband to take out the trash. All she has stated is the what. We are also going to paint more of the picture; the husband is watching the football game when he is asked to take out the trash.

Several hours pass and the trash still hasn't been taken out. The wife starts getting angry but is still composed. The second game of the day comes and goes, and the wife is now furious. "Why is he taking so long to take out the trash? Did he not hear me? Does he not care?"

Now, the game ends and she confronts him, angrily, explodes in a fit of rage over something so simple as taking out the garbage.

Well, the request was simple but it lacked all communication of the underlying expectations, and the husband not following those unknown expectations is what made her angry. What she could have said is, "Honey, could you take out the trash now?" By simply adding the word now, she is setting an expectation of timing. The what and when. She is at a minimum communicating some of her expectations.

She could have taken it a bit further and said, "Honey, could you take out the trash now. It is starting to stink up the place." She is now setting the expectation of what, when, and why.

When you can get out the What, When, and Why, you are clearly stating an expectation so that everyone is aware of those expectations. They become known. At that point, the husband could negotiate because he may have his own expectations. Like, being able to watch the games without being asked to do anything.

This brings us to an important point.

Let's take a step back to the first example. Perhaps the wife didn't know she had an expectation and started getting angry. **Well, the only reason anyone ever gets upset is because an expectation hasn't been met.**

This means that as soon as she started to feel angry, she could have stopped herself and explored why. She could be asking herself, what expectation isn't being met? Did I know I had that expectation until this very moment?

Guess what!? **Most people don't know they have an expectation until they are upset.** And as soon as you realize you had an unknown expectation, you can go back to rule number one! Don't Deny! Don't deny that you had an unknown (or known) expectation. Don't deny that you never shared that expectation. Don't deny that until you share the expectation, nothing can be done by the other party to fulfil those expectations (or negotiate those expectations).

This is your opportunity to move through the first rule and on to rule number two. Now you can "yes, and" the situation and share the newly found expectation to those involved. As soon as the wife got upset, she could take a step back and share more details rather than get upset. "Honey, I asked you to take the trash out and I didn't tell you that I would like it done now because it stinks. Could you take it out now?"

Doesn't that seem like a better approach than yelling, getting angry, and stressed out?

The best way to avoid ever being upset is to provide as many expectations (information) as possible before hand. And the second best is to realize you are getting upset, take a step back, and examine what expectation is being missed. By realizing you had an expectation, you can then add information, you can "yes, and" the situation and move forward in a positive and effective way.

For those who are still trying to figure out how there is a way to be upset, without there being an underlying expectation that isn't being met, I look forward to having solid proof that makes me wrong ;-)

If you're sick and upset about it, you had an expectation of being well.

If someone close to you dies and you are upset about it, you had an expectation that they would be around longer. Or you had an expectation of being able to tell them how you felt before they died. Or any number of expectations.

Regret is often an unrealized expectation.

If you didn't get the girl/guy you wanted, you had an expectation of being chosen.

If you go to the store and you are upset because they are out of what you want to buy, you had an expectation of the product being available.

If you think traffic should move better and everyone should be better drivers, and you wonder how they got their license in the first place, and there should be more rules and checkups for drivers, and traffic just flat out upsets you, you have unrealistic expectations...yes, this is the one I struggle with on a daily basis. Even I have expectations that I work through.

Basically, anything that makes you upset, there is the opposite side of the equation where you had an expectation of how it was supposed to be. Sometimes you can *"yes, and"* the situation with someone else to remedy the situation, and sometimes you simply have to "accept what is" and realize the situation isn't going to change. At that point you get to figure out how to make the best out of it. *"Yes, and,"* can be as simple as making the best out of a situation that is out of your control. It is where you can only control your attitude surrounding the situation.

At this point you can start to see how intertwined the first three rules are. When an expectation isn't being met, you can start with rule number one and "accept that you are upset." From there you can take steps (*yes, and*) to figure out a solution. By adding to, you can *be specific* in what you want, change the expectation, communicate the expectation, and so on. In any situation, you can move back and forth and through all three rules in just moments. You could run through all three rules in the matter of seconds. It is easy to do with practice.

The best point to start practicing is when you notice you are upset. **Being upset is the most recognizable point that one or more of these rules aren't being followed.**

To notice you are upset you must…

Here it comes…

You're not ready for this. Are you?

Sure you are!

Go for it!

Turn the page!

Chapter 9

Rule #4
Focus on the Present

The Fourth Rule of Improv – Focus on the Present

…focus on the present. The fourth rule of improv, *Focus on the Present*, is so important in performance improv. If you are thinking about anything else, chores, a due date, how someone reacted at work today, your bank account, while participating in the scene, you will miss what was said or done. You won't be able to play along. This is just as detrimental as "denial" or "yes, but". It is the opposite of productive. It is the opposite of helpful. It is impossible to *"yes, and"* effectively if you weren't present enough to be involved in the first place.

Let's say actor one says, "…and then we went to into the cave and the lights stopped working." The actor who wasn't paying attention could end up saying, "Yeah, cooking in the dark sucks. Especially since our kitchen isn't laid out like normal kitchens." The actor tries to *"yes, and"* the scene having only heard that the lights went out. They even attempt to *be specific* about it, however, they weren't aware they were talking about a cave and not their kitchen. Now, EVERYONE is confused. The scene is effectively dead. May as well stop there and end the show. *There are ways to recover from this, and that's advanced improv. That takes years of practice.* If you are focused on the present, you can help provide information to the other person who doesn't have all of their facts in order. The best negotiators in the world are present in those negotiations. They are so focused on the present that they hear what is spoken, see what isn't spoken, and respond effectively. They can *"yes, and"* the negotiation to the point where the other person comes up with the final solution on their own and that solution works out for everyone. At that point, they have bought in so heavily that they won't change their mind later, because they already changed their mind.

Car salesmen are a prime example. You may have gone in to check a car out and they *"yes, and"* you to the point where you leave with a car you weren't expecting to buy. And by the end of the day, it was your idea to move forward with buying it rather than it being their idea. Ultimately they wanted you to buy, and they made it happen in such a way that you bought it based on your decision.

Some may call this manipulation, and yes, it is possible to use these rules in a manipulative way, but that is not the intent here. If you choose to use these rules for manipulation, that is your karma. Good luck with that.

By *being present*, by focusing on the here and now, you gain freedom. Freedom from worry, because we do not tend to worry about the present. We worry about the future. Freedom from fear, because we are usually fearful of what might happen in the future. Freedom from regret, because what is past is past and unchangeable anyway, no matter how much we may want to. You are able to just be in the moment, like a kid playing with their toys. Nothing else matters at that moment. We can only change what is here and now in the present. Thus *Focus on the Present*.

How about being on a date? Do you think you'll get another date if you never listen to what is being said because you are thinking about other things?

No way! You're date may end before you realize it.

By the way, getting on your phone while on a date is exactly the same thing, unless you set the expectation that you might be getting an important call.

Do you believe that your husband will feel respected if you are focused on work while he is sharing his difficulties? Or vice versa?

How many couples have a fight with the phrase, "Are you even listening to me?"

The reality is that this rule is about building a relationship in a positive way. It is about understanding. It is about being present so that all information is accurately heard and understood. With being present, you can respond rather than react. With being present, you can see if one of the previous rules is being followed, skipped, or needs to be reapplied.

When you *focus on the present* and let go of regret and worry, people begin to realize you are focused and they can rely on you to be present. Also, you can rely on yourself more.

In other words you create and now

have….

Chapter 10

Rule #5

Trust

The Fifth Rule of Improv – Trust

The fifth rule of improv isn't necessarily a rule, but a result of having followed the other four rules. By following the previous four rules you create *trust*. The more often those rules are followed, the stronger the *trust*.

You CAN think of it as a rule. There should be *trust* out of the gate. Not blind trust. Not trust just to trust. You do have to follow your intuition. The rule of *trust* is around intuition, your gut feeling. Listening to your intuition is the ultimate *trust*. Your intuition will never lie to you. Trusting the weird psychotic looking guy in a dark ally, probably not a good idea. Trusting your intuition about that guy is a good idea.

In performance improv, usually a troupe of improv artists will work together for a long period of time.

They learn each other's habits, ideas, processes, actions. They learn who follows the rules and how they follow the rules. When they bend those rules and so on. As time goes on, they all develop *trust* with each other. The stronger the *trust* in the troupe, the better the performances.

This is no different in real life improv. The more you and those around you follow the rules together, the stronger the *trust*. The more fun everyone is having. Less fighting. More understanding. More teamwork. More innovation. Better work environment.

Trust in relationships is huge. Both giving *trust* and feeling *trust*. Who likes to be told what to do? Nobody. Who likes to tell people what to do? Some might, but this usually stems from a lack of *trust* and an abundance of worry. Ultimately nobody likes to deal with the little things. There is no *trust* when everything is questioned. Both directions. Your wife doesn't feel like they are trusted to do the task. The husband doesn't *trust* that his wife is able to do their task. That is a downward spiral. It is ineffective. Just think of the previous rules and how many of them are broken just by micro-managing/being micro-managed.

By being *trust*ed to do a task, you want to reward that *trust* by doing the best job possible. By *trust*ing someone to do their task, you are going to empower them and get better results. More respect. Everyone wins.

Understanding leads to *trust*. *Trust* leads to happiness. Happiness leads to love.

The first four rules create understanding and *trust*. The rest falls into place.

Think of the people in your life who you *trust* completely. You would follow them into the heart of a dangerous situation. You would leave your kids to them if you died. You would hand over all of your money because you *trust* them enough to know they won't harm you or those you care about.

Now, think of how the previous rules are implemented with that person. *Trust* at that level was earned by following the previous four rules. Even if you didn't know about it, in reflection, you can probably see how those rules were applied.

But…But…

Yes, everyone has THAT But…

No…not that butt!

This but…

Chapter 11

What if I am the only…

The biggest question everyone has at this point is, "What if I am the only one following these rules?" And that is a great question.

Let me ask you a simple question. Who do you talk with the most? Yourself. Yes, you have a relationship with yourself. You have more dialog with yourself than anyone else. It's true. Talking to yourself is totally acceptable and encouraged, as long as it is in a loving way. How do the rules of improv apply to you talking with yourself? The same way they would if you were talking with someone else.

Do you get upset with yourself? Do you have expectations of yourself? Of course you do. "I'm going to go to the gym every day this week." And then you don't. "I'm going to stick to this diet." And then you don't. "I'm going to keep the house clean." Didn't happen. "I'm going to write that book I always wanted to write." Decided TV was better. "I'm going to…" And so on.

You had an expectation of yourself and you didn't follow through. Now you are upset with yourself. Well, stop it. This is the point where you get to *"accept what is"* with your situation. To *"yes, and"* yourself. To be specific with yourself. To *focus on the present*. What can you do at this moment to make the situation better?

The rules of improv work for individual conversations just as much as they do with other relationships. Isn't *trust*ing yourself just as important as *trust*ing others? Doesn't *trust*ing yourself lead to loving yourself? And isn't that important?

How do interactions with others work when you know the rules and they don't? This is tricky. It involves understanding. It involves knowing that they don't know the rules and adjusting yourself in that situation. You simply cannot change anyone else. Only yourself. You have heard this before and it is no different now. How you react in a situation is all you can control. Remember, if you are getting upset in the situation, you can only check in with yourself and see if you are communicating effectively. To see if you have shared your expectations. You, by knowing the rules, get to play the game. The other people around you are just on the field wandering about. And while this may be frustrating at times, you will actually find humor where others don't because you know which rule isn't being followed.

Because you know how easy it can be to switch the situation to not suck. Fun becomes the norm.

When you follow the rules of improv, everything works better. You now have the rules of the game. You know how to win. To have fun. To Thrive. To be SUCCESSFUL!!!

Now, go forth and play! Love! Be Happy!

Appendix A: Dating

Dating is one big wild game of improv. You meet characters of all kinds while dating. If you had expectations of how someone should be when you meet them, stop now. Just follow the rules of improv and all of your dates will be "fun". They may not go as you hope, but with understanding, rather than frustration, you can actually get better at picking the desired traits in what you are looking for. Focus on the present is huge for dating.

Might I recommend leaving your phone in the car when you meet your date for the first time? Hint Hint.

Appendix B: Conflict Resolution

The above rules, when followed, stop conflict before it even starts. But since we are all human, it is sometimes necessary for people to remind each other of the rules. Conflict usually means that someone is upset. Or both people are upset. And what does that mean? Being upset is the trigger that should say in your mind, "STOP. Follow the rules now." Conflict is typically resolved quickly when the situation is diffused. By following Rule number 1, it is almost immediately diffused.

"You know...you're right. I screwed up." It takes the edge out of the argument quickly. And from there, the rest of the rules can be followed.

Following the rules fosters communication and understanding. Two things necessary for conflict resolution.

Appendix C: General Energy

People are always looking for ways to increase or change their energy. The rules and foundation set in this book foster a change of thought, energy, communication, and understanding. And when you can think differently, actually communicate effectively, and understand others, everyone around you feels valued and you feel good about you. Now…doesn't that just scream an increase and change of energy? Doesn't that sound like a place you want to be?

Appendix D: Long-Term Relationships

Most people learn to communicate from their parents, who may or may not be experts. Mostly likely they learned some things that are effective and sometimes they learned some things that the world could do without.

When in a long-term relationship we often revert to the programming/habits we learned from our parents without even thinking about it. This doesn't always foster the trust factor that is needed in the success of a long-term relationship.

The rules in this book offer a unified approach to better and effective communication. Half of communication is listening and being present. Two things taught in this book.

Don't Deny

Yes, And…

Be Specific

Focus on the Present

Trust

Learn how to succeed with classes from

SuccessImprov.com